Tennessee

by Patricia K. Kummer,
Capstone Press
Geography Department

Content Consultant:
Bruce Opic
Executive Director for Curriculum and Instruction
Tennessee Department of Education

C A P S T O N E
H I G H / L O W B O O K S
an imprint of Capstone Press

C A P S T O N E   P R E S S

818 North Willow Street • Mankato, MN 56001

http://www.capstone-press.com

Library of Congress Cataloging-in-Publication Data
Kummer, Patricia K.
    Tennessee/by Patricia K. Kummer; Capstone Press Geography Department.
       p. cm. -- (One nation)
    Includes bibliographical references and index.
    Summary: An overview of the state of Tennessee, including its history,
geography, people, and living conditions.
    ISBN 1-56065-681-6
    1. Tennessee--Juvenile literature. [1. Tennessee.] I. Capstone Press. Geography
Dept. II. Title. III. Series.
F436.3.K86 1998
976.8--dc21
                          97-40820
                             CIP
                             AC

Editorial Credits:
Editor, Martha E. Hillman; cover design and illustrations, Timothy Halldin; photo
  research, Michelle L. Norstad

Photo Credits:
International Stock/Chad Ehlers, cover
Charles W. Melton, 4 (bottom)
One Mile Up, Inc., 4 (top)
Root Resources, D & I MacDonald, 33
Cheyenne Rouse, 10
James P. Rowan, 20, 23, 26
Unicorn Stock Photos/Doris Brookes, 5 (top); Robin Rudd, 5 (bottom), 25; Jean
  Higgins, 6, 37; Dennis MacDonald, 9; Martha McBride, 14; Florent Flipper, 16;
  Arni Katz, 29; Andre Jenny, 30; Scott Liles, 34

Table of Contents

Fast Facts about Tennessee

State Flag

Location: In the southeastern United States

Size: 42,244 square miles (109,834 square kilometers)

Population: 5,307,381 (1996 U.S. Census Bureau estimate)

Capital: Nashville

Date admitted to the Union: June 1, 1796; the 16th state

Mockingbird

Iris

Largest cities:
Memphis,
Nashville,
Knoxville,
Chattanooga,
Clarksville,
Johnson City,
Jackson,
Murfreesboro,
Kingsport,
Germantown

Nickname: The
Volunteer State
State animal:
Raccoon
State bird:
Mockingbird
State flower: Iris
State tree:
Tulip poplar
State songs:

Tulip poplar

"My Homeland, Tennessee," "When It's Iris
Time in Tennessee," "My Tennessee,"
"The Tennessee Waltz," and "Rocky Top"

Chapter 1

Music, Music, Music

Many Tennesseans love music. Tennessee is the only state with five state songs.

East Tennessee is known for folk music. Country music is popular in Middle Tennessee. Early blues and rock and roll flourished in West Tennessee. The blues is a kind of music that often addresses sad or unhappy feelings. It began in the early 1900s.

Folk Music

Tennessee's folk music dates to the 1700s. Early settlers brought old English songs with them. Over the years, East Tennesseans have passed these songs down.

Early rock and roll flourished in Memphis and East Tennessee.

Some folk songs tell stories of everyday life. Others are meant for dancing. People play many folk songs on guitars, fiddles, and banjos.

Music City, USA

Nashville is called Music City, USA. People also call it the Capital of Country Music.

Music Row is a section of Nashville. Recording studios line the streets there. Country music stars like Garth Brooks and Barbara Mandrell have made albums there. The Country Music Hall of Fame is in Music Row, too. The Hall of Fame honors country music stars.

Nashville also has a huge music theme park. It is called Opryland USA. The Grand Ole Opry House is in the park. Country music stars perform there. People around the nation can watch these performances on television.

Blues and Rock and Roll

W. C. Handy came to Beale Street in Memphis in 1903. He started writing blues songs. They were based on African American songs. The songs "Memphis Blues" and "Beale Street

Blues" made Handy famous. Today, he is known as the Father of the Blues.

Elvis Presley made his first record a few blocks from Beale Street. He made the record at Sun Studio in 1954. Presley's music combined blues and country music. His recordings sold millions of copies in the 1950s and 1960s. Some people call Presley the King of Rock and Roll. Presley died in 1977. Every year, about 600,000 people visit Graceland. This was Presley's mansion in Memphis.

Every year, about 600,000 people visit Graceland.

Chapter 2

The Land

Tennessee is in the southeastern United States. Mississippi, Georgia, and Alabama lie south of Tennessee. Kentucky and Virginia are to the north. North Carolina is to the east. Arkansas and Missouri are to the west.

Tennessee is a long, narrow state. It reaches from the Appalachian Mountains to the Mississippi River. The state's lowest point is along this river. This point is 178 feet (54 meters) above sea level. Sea level is the average level of the ocean's surface.

There are three stars on Tennessee's state flag. They stand for the three parts of Tennessee. These parts are East Tennessec,

Some of the Appalachian Mountains are in Tennessee.

Middle Tennessee, and West Tennessee. Each part of the state has a different kind of land.

East Tennessee

The Appalachian Mountains form Tennessee's far eastern edge. The Great Smoky Mountains is a range in the Appalachians. Clingmans Dome is a mountain in this range. It is Tennessee's highest point. It stands 6,643 feet (2,025 meters) above sea level.

The Appalachian Ridge and Valley Region is west of the Appalachians. This series of

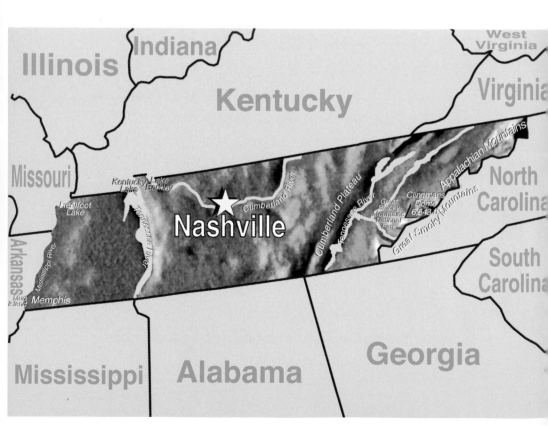

mountains and valleys contains rich farmland. Knoxville is in this part of Tennessee. It is the state's third-largest city.

The Cumberland Plateau is west of the valley. Flat-topped mountains and deep valleys cover this area.

Middle Tennessee

The Highland Rim covers much of Middle Tennessee. High plains make up the Highland Rim. There are caves under much of this land.

The Central Basin sits in the center of the Highland Rim. The basin has rich farmland. Tobacco and wheat grow well in this basin.

Nashville is in the Central Basin. This is Tennessee's capital. It is also the state's second largest city.

West Tennessee

West Tennessee is part of the Gulf Coastal Plain. Flat, low land covers the plain. Some of Tennessee's best farmland is there. Farmers raise soybeans and cotton in this area.

Memphis is in West Tennessee. It is the state's largest city.

Reelfoot Lake is Tennessee's largest natural lake.

Rivers and Lakes

The Mississippi River forms Tennessee's entire western border. The Cumberland River winds across northern Middle Tennessee.

The Tennessee River flows south through East Tennessee into Alabama. Then it turns north and flows back into West Tennessee.

People made most of Tennessee's lakes when they built dams on rivers. The water in the rivers backed up to form lakes. Kentucky Lake is the largest of these lakes.

Reelfoot Lake is the state's largest natural lake. It formed after earthquakes struck Tennessee during the winter of 1811-1812. Water from the Mississippi River flowed into a low area created by the earthquakes.

Wildlife

Black bears and wild hogs live in Tennessee's mountains. Bass and trout swim in its lakes and rivers.

Many animals live near Reelfoot Lake. Bald eagles spend winters there. Otters and beavers live in the lake. White-tailed deer, great blue herons, and ospreys live near the lake.

Climate

Tennessee has a mild climate throughout the year. Temperatures in Tennessee range from 31 degrees Fahrenheit (-0.5 degrees Celsius) to 90 degrees Fahrenheit (32 degrees Celsius).

Tennessee's mountains receive more snow than the rest of Tennessee. Middle Tennessee receives the most rain. Tennessee receives about 50 inches (127 centimeters) of rain and snow each year.

Chapter 3

The People

Tennessee has the 17th largest population among the states. It is a fast-growing state. Between 1990 and 1995, Tennessee's population grew by almost 400,000 people.

Many people moved to Tennessee from northern states. Some retired in Tennessee. They liked the state's mild climate.

More than 60 percent of Tennesseans live in or near large cities. More than 600,000 people live in Memphis. Nashville, Knoxville, Chattanooga, and Clarksville also have large populations.

Almost 40 percent of Tennesseans live in rural areas. Rural means away from large cities. Rural Tennesseans live on farms or in small towns.

Nashville is one of Tennessee's largest cities.

Early Settlers

Tennessee's first white settlers arrived during the 1770s. They came from Pennsylvania, Virginia, and North Carolina. Most settlers had English, Scottish, Irish, or German backgrounds. A few had French backgrounds.

The earliest settlers lived between the Watauga and Nolichucky Rivers. In 1806, settlers founded Nashville in Middle Tennessee. Settlers moved into West Tennessee by 1820.

Today, about 83 percent of Tennesseans have European backgrounds. Many are relatives of Tennessee's early settlers.

African Americans

The first African Americans in Tennessee were slaves. Settlers from Virginia and North Carolina brought slaves to Tennessee. African American slaves worked in tobacco fields. They planted and picked cotton in West Tennessee.

By 1860, more than 250,000 slaves lived in Tennessee. About 7,300 free African Americans also lived there. In 1865, all African Americans in the nation gained their freedom.

Today, about 800,000 Tennesseans are African Americans. Most live in West Tennessee. About 55 percent of the people in Memphis are African American. In 1991, Willie Herenton became the first African American mayor of Memphis.

Other Ethnic Groups

About one percent of Tennesseans belong to other ethnic groups. They are Hispanic Americans, Asian Americans, and Native Americans.

Memphis, Nashville, and Chattanooga have growing Hispanic populations. Many of these Hispanic Americans have Mexican or Puerto Rican backgrounds.

Knoxville, Nashville, and Memphis have growing Asian American populations. Many of these Asian Americans have Chinese, Indian, or Korean backgrounds.

Most of Tennessee's Native Americans are Cherokees or Chickasaws. Many of the Cherokees live in East Tennessee. West Tennessee is home to most Chickasaws.

Chapter 4

Tennessee History

People have lived in the area that is now Tennessee for about 15,000 years. Native Americans were the first people in Tennessee. By 1500, Cherokees had villages in today's East and Middle Tennessee. Creeks lived in the southeast. Chickasaws were living in present-day West Tennessee.

English and French Claims

By the 1600s, England and France claimed land in North America. This included the land that is now Tennessee.

The two countries fought for control of North America during the French and Indian War (1754-1763). The Creeks helped the

Some Native Americans built huts like this in Tennessee.

French. Cherokees and Chickasaws helped the English.

In 1763, France gave up its land east of the Mississippi River. The area that is now Tennessee became part of North Carolina. North Carolina was one of England's 13 American colonies.

The Revolutionary War

In 1769, American colonists started settling in the Tennessee area. By 1780, about 10,000 people lived there.

The Revolutionary War began in 1775. North Carolina and the other colonies fought England for their independence. People from present-day Tennessee fought in the war. In 1780, these soldiers fought a major battle in South Carolina. This was the Battle of Kings Mountain.

The colonies won the Revolutionary War in 1783. They became a new country called the United States of America.

The Volunteer State

Tennesseans wanted their own state. By 1796, Tennessee had 80,000 people. That was enough to become a state. In 1796, Tennessee entered the Union as the 16th state.

England attacked the United States during the War of 1812 (1812-1815). Andrew Jackson led Tennessee soldier volunteers to New Orleans. A volunteer is someone who offers to do a job. These volunteers fought and defeated English forces there.

The colonists who settled the Tennessee area in the late 1700s wore clothing similar to this.

People called Tennessee the Volunteer State after the War of 1812. Since that war, many Tennesseans have volunteered to fight in other wars.

The Mid-1800s

By 1839, the U.S. government had forced Native Americans out of Tennessee. The Native Americans travelled to the land that is now Oklahoma. Their route was called the Trail of Tears. Many people died during the trip. Settlers moved to the Tennessee area.

Tennessee grew quickly. By 1850, more than one million people lived in the state. Cotton, tobacco, and corn fields covered the state. Railroads crossed Tennessee.

Slavery and Civil War

The issue of slavery divided the nation and Tennessee. Many Northerners did not think people should own other people. Slavery was illegal in Northern states. Southerners wanted to decide for themselves. The Southern states allowed slavery.

Cotton fields covered Tennessee by 1850.

In Middle and West Tennessee, slaves worked on plantations. A plantation is a large farm. Few East Tennesseans had slaves. Those Tennesseans sided with the Northern states.

Eleven southern states seceded from the Union. Secede means to break away from a group. The states formed a new country called the Confederate States of America. This led to the Civil War (1861-1865). Tennessee seceded

More than 200 Civil War battles took place in Tennessee.

after the war had started. It was the last of the eleven Southern states to secede.

About 125,000 Tennesseans fought for the Confederacy. Almost 70,000 Tennesseans fought for the Union. More than 200 Civil War battles took place in Tennessee.

The Confederacy surrendered on April 9, 1865. A few days later, John Wilkes Booth killed President Abraham Lincoln. Tennessean Andrew Johnson became president of the United States.

Rebuilding Tennessee

The Civil War destroyed Tennessee farms, factories, and railroads. Tennesseans worked to rebuild their state. In 1866, Tennessee became the first state allowed to rejoin the Union.

By the early 1900s, Tennessee was growing again. Cotton and woolen mills went up around the state. More coal mines opened in East Tennessee.

World Wars and Depression

In 1917, the United States entered World War I (1914-1918). Tennessee workers made cotton and woolen cloth for soldiers' uniforms. Many soldiers from Tennessee helped the United States win the war.

During the Great Depression (1929-1939), factories and mines closed all over the United States. The Great Depression was a period of national hardship. Thousands of Tennesseans lost their jobs. In 1933, the U.S. government started the Tennessee Valley Authority (TVA). The TVA was a work program. Workers with the TVA built dams on Tennessee rivers. Many Tennesseans worked on these dams.

In 1941, the United States entered World War II (1939-1945). The government built Oak Ridge, Tennessee, as a secret city. Scientists at Oak Ridge National Laboratories helped develop the atomic bomb. An atomic bomb is a powerful explosive that destroys large areas. It leaves behind harmful elements. This new weapon helped end World War II.

Recent Growth
Tennessee grew after World War II. It now has one of the fastest-growing economies in the

South. Businesses from northern states have moved to Tennessee. East Tennessee has several computer plants. Middle Tennessee has many auto plants.

Tennessee's largest cities have rebuilt their downtowns. Many tourists visit these cities. In the 1990s, Tennesseans started programs to improve their schools. They are also working to improve health care in the state.

Workers with the TVA built dams on Tennessee rivers.

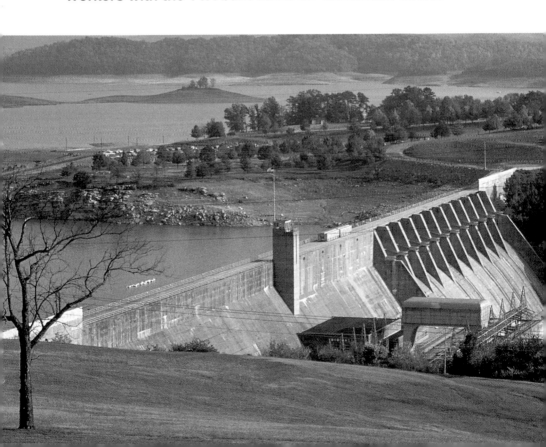

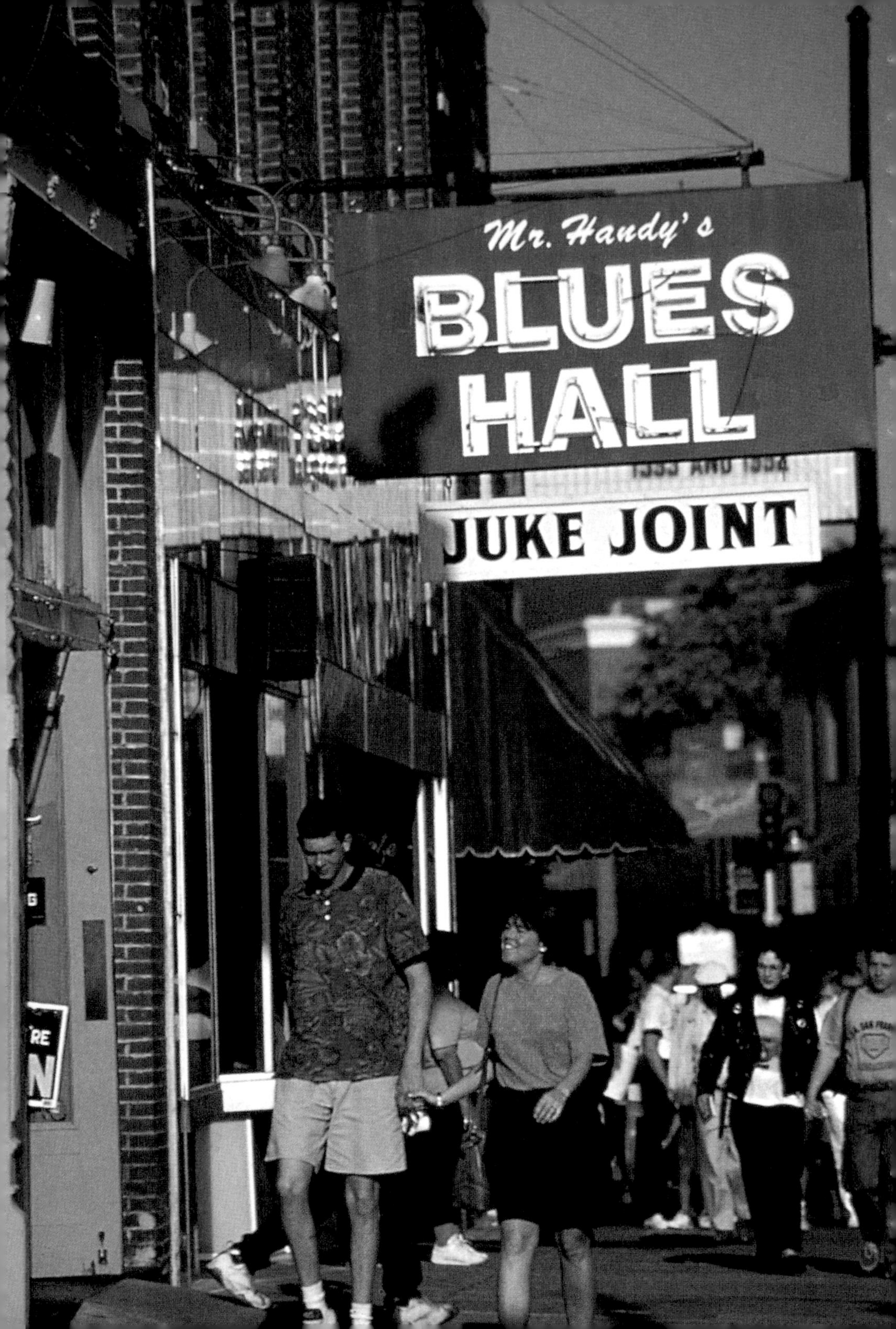

Mr. Handy's
BLUES
HALL
JUKE JOINT

Chapter 5

Tennessee Business

Manufacturing is Tennessee's most valuable business. Service businesses are also important. Service businesses include trade, government, and tourism. Many tourists come to Tennessee for its music. Farming and mining are other Tennessee businesses.

Manufacturing

Tennessee's leading product is machinery used for heating and cooling. Trucks and cars are other important products. Nissan has an auto factory in Smyrna. General Motors builds Saturn cars in Spring Hill.

Tennessee factories make paint, medicine, and soap. Memphis workers bake bread and make cereal. Chattanooga has large flour mills.

Many tourists come to Tennessee for its music.

Northeastern Tennessee has paper mills and printing plants. Nashville companies are among the world's leading publishers of Bibles.

Service Businesses

Trade is Tennessee's leading service business. Memphis is the nation's largest center for trading raw cotton. Trade is also important in Nashville, Chattanooga, and Knoxville. All four cities have large river ports.

Tourism is another important service business. Tourists spend about $5 billion a year in Tennessee. Hotels, music halls, and museums earn much of this money.

Many Tennesseans work for the U.S. government. Some operate dams for the TVA. Others work at Oak Ridge National Laboratories.

Agriculture

Farmland covers about half of Tennessee. Beef cattle and milk are the state's leading farm goods. Middle Tennessee has many horse farms. Farmers raise Tennessee walking horses on them. The Tennessee walking horse is a breed known for its smooth walk.

Agriculture is an important Tennessee business.

Cotton is Tennessee's leading crop. Tobacco, soybeans, hay, and corn are other important crops.

Mining

Coal is Tennessee's leading mining product. Many coal mines are located in East Tennessee.

Tennessee companies also mine zinc and limestone. East Tennessee leads the nation in mining zinc.

Chapter 6

Seeing the Sights

Tennessee has many historic sites, including old battlefields. People visit its large cities. Visitors also enjoy outdoor activities in the state's lakes and mountains. Some people come to Tennessee to see music performances.

Memphis

Memphis is in far southwestern Tennessee. It lies on the Mississippi River.

Mud Island is in the middle of the river across from Memphis. The Mississippi River Museum is on the island. Exhibits display the history of life along the Mississippi.

A train takes visitors from the island into downtown Memphis. The National Civil Rights

Memphis lies on the Mississippi River.

Museum is south of the downtown area. It is in the Lorraine Motel. James Earl Ray killed civil rights leader Martin Luther King Jr. there in 1968. The museum's exhibits trace the story of the civil rights movement.

Other West Tennessee Sights

The Alex Haley House Museum is in Henning. Visitors tour the home of the author of *Roots*. This book traces Haley's family back to Africa.

Shiloh National Military Park is southeast of Henning. A major Civil War battle took place there in 1862. Today, visitors drive through the battlefield.

Nashville

Nashville is in Middle Tennessee. It is called the Athens of the South. Some of its buildings look like the ancient buildings of Athens, Greece. The state capitol was also built in Greek style.

The Parthenon stands in Centennial Park. The Parthenon was a temple in Athens, Greece. Nashville's Parthenon is a museum.

The Hermitage is just east of Nashville. President Andrew Jackson built this Greek-style house. Visitors tour the house.

Other Middle Tennessee Sights

The Land Between the Lakes is northwest of Nashville. Kentucky Lake and Lake Barkley are located here. Part of this area extends into Kentucky.

Stones River National Battlefield is southeast of Nashville. In 1863, the Union won an important battle there.

Shelbyville is home to the Tennessee Walking Horse Museum. Visitors learn about the history of this famous breed of horse.

The Parthenon stands in Nashville's Centennial Park.

Chattanooga

Chattanooga is in the far southern part of East Tennessee. It is home to the Tennessee Aquarium. This is the world's largest freshwater aquarium. A major exhibit features wildlife of the Tennessee River.

Mountains surround Chattanooga. One of them is Lookout Mountain. In 1863, the Union won the Battle above the Clouds on Lookout Mountain. Today, the Lookout Mountain Incline Railway takes visitors to the battlefield.

Other East Tennessee Sights

Knoxville is home to the University of Tennessee. About 27,000 students attend classes there. The university calls its sports teams the Volunteers.

The city of Pigeon Forge is southeast of Knoxville. Country singer Dolly Parton owns a theme park there called Dollywood. It features rides, music, and crafts.

Great Smoky Mountains National Park is east of Dollywood. This is the country's most-visited national park. More than 9 million people visited the park in 1995. Many people hike, camp, and fish in its wooded mountains. Others simply drive through the park to enjoy the scenery.

Tennessee Time Line

About 13,000 B.C.—People are living in the Tennessee area.

1500—Cherokee, Chickasaw, and Creek people are living in present-day Tennessee.

1673—English and French explorers enter the Tennessee area.

1714—French traders set up a trading post near present-day Nashville.

1763—France gives up land east of the Mississippi River to England; present-day Tennessee becomes part of North Carolina.

1789—The U.S. government forms the Tennessee Territory when North Carolina turns over the land to the government.

1796—Tennessee becomes the 16th state.

1811-1812—Reelfoot Lake forms after earthquakes strike Tennessee.

1818—The Chickasaws sell their land in West Tennessee to the U.S. government.

1838—The U.S. government forces the Cherokees from their land in East Tennessee; they travel the Trail of Tears to Oklahoma.

1861—The Civil War starts in April; Tennessee is the last of 11 states to leave the Union.

1865—The Civil War ends; Tennessean Andrew Johnson becomes the U.S. president after John Wilkes Booth kills President Lincoln.

1866—Tennessee is the first southern state allowed to rejoin the Union.

1878—Yellow fever kills more than 5,000 people in Memphis.

1933—The Tennessee Valley Authority begins building dams in Tennessee.

1942—Workers at Oak Ridge National Laboratory begin work on the atomic bomb.

1956—Desegregation of Tennessee schools begins.

1968—James Earl Ray kills Dr. Martin Luther King Jr. in Memphis.

1972—Opryland USA opens in Nashville.

1990—General Motors opens a Saturn automobile plant in Spring Hill.

1991—Willie Herenton is elected as the first African American mayor of Memphis.

1996—Tennessee celebrates its 200th birthday as a state.

1997—The University of Tennessee women's basketball team wins the NCAA championship for the third time in seven years.

Famous Tennesseans

Davy Crockett (1786-1836) Politician and soldier who served Tennessee in the U.S. House of Representatives; born in Limestone.

Aretha Franklin (1942-) Gospel singer who became the Queen of Soul Music; known for singing the song "Respect"; born in Memphis.

Albert Gore, Jr. (1948-) Lawyer and politician who served Tennessee in the U.S. House of Representatives and in the U.S. Senate; vice president of the United States (1993-); born in Washington, D.C.; moved to Nashville in 1971.

Andrew Jackson (1767-1845) Politician who was president of the United States (1829-1837); born in South Carolina and moved to Nashville in 1787; built an estate called the Hermitage.

Andrew Johnson (1808-1875) Tennessee politician who became president after Abraham Lincoln's death; born in Raleigh, North Carolina.

Dolly Parton (1946-) Singer, songwriter, and actress; owns the Dollywood theme park in Pigeon Forge; born in Sevierville.

Elvis Presley (1935-1977) Singer who made rock and roll music popular; born in Tupelo, Mississippi; moved to Memphis in 1948; lived in a mansion called Graceland from 1957 to 1977.

Sequoya (1760?-1843) Scholar who invented the Cherokee alphabet, the first alphabet for a Native American language; born in Taskigi in East Tennessee.

Cybill Shepherd (1950-) Actress and singer who starred in *The Last Picture Show* and in the television shows *Moonlighting* and *Cybill*; born in Memphis.

Ida B. Wells (1862-1931) Memphis teacher who worked for civil rights; born a slave in Mississippi and moved to Memphis in 1884.

Words to Know

atomic bomb (uh-TOM-ik BOM)—a powerful explosive that destroys large areas; it leaves behind harmful elements

blues (BLOOZ)— a kind of music that often addresses sad or unhappy feelings

plantation (plan-TAY-shuhn)—a large farm

rural (RUR-uhl)—away from large cities

sea level (SEE LEV-uhl)—the average level of the ocean's surface

secede (si-SEED)—to break away from a group

volunteer (vol-uhn-TIHR)—someone who offers to do a job

To Learn More

Aylesworth, Thomas G. and Virginia L. Aylesworth. *The Southeast: Georgia, Kentucky, Tennessee*. New York: Chelsea House Publishers, 1995.

Fradin, Dennis Brindell. *Tennessee*. From Sea to Shining Sea. Chicago: Children's Press, 1992.

Thompson, Kathleen. *Tennessee*. Austin: Raintree Steck-Vaughn Publishers, 1996.

Wilcox, Charlotte. *The Tennessee Walking Horse*. Mankato, Minn.: Capstone Press, 1996.

Internet Sites

Blues Tour
http://www.memphisguide.com/music2/
   bluestour/blues.html/blues1.html

Excite Travel: Tennessee, United States
http://www.city.net/countries/united_states/
   tennessee/

Opryland USA
http://www.country.com/usa/usa-f.html

TRAVEL.org—Tennessee
http://travel.org/tennesse.html

Welcome to Tennessee.net
http://www.tennessee.net/

Useful Addresses

Alex Haley House Museum
200 South Church Street
Henning, TN 38041

Graceland
3734 Elvis Presley Boulevard
Memphis, TN 38186

Great Smoky Mountains National Park
Sugarlands Visitors Center
U.S. 441
Gatlinburg, TN 37738

**Tennessee Department of
   Tourist Development**
320 Sixth Avenue North
5th Floor, Rachel Jackson Building
Nashville, TN 37243

Index